About the Author

Darren Cox was born in south-east London in 1981 where he still lives. He was a happy, outgoing and popular child who dreamed of growing up to be a professional footballer. His life didn't turn out the way he expected, but he's the proud father of three wonderful children and has a kind, supportive and understanding family and group of friends around him. He's dealt with mental health issues his entire adult life and now wants to tell his story to help other young men in a similar situation.

Lion Heart

Darren Cox

Lion Heart

Olympia Publishers
London

www.olympiapublishers.com
OLYMPIA PAPERBACK EDITION

A CIP catalogue record for this title is
available from the British Library.

ISBN: 978-1-80074-059-4

This is a work of fiction.
Names, characters, places and incidents originate from the writer's
imagination. Any resemblance to actual persons, living or dead, is
purely coincidental.

First Published in 2021

Olympia Publishers
Tallis House
2 Tallis Street
London
EC4Y 0AB

Printed in Great Britain

My Depression

My name is Darren, and I am a thirty-seven-year-old who has struggled with depression for the past nineteen years.

When I was first diagnosed all those years ago, there was a massive stigma about mental health.

I was so embarrassed to admit I had depression. I wouldn't talk to anyone for days on end. In the early days, I would lock myself away in my room for weeks and months at a time. Only coming out for food, drink and medication.

I used to cut myself off from the outside world. I would switch my phone off and hide from the outside world. No contact with family and friends what so ever. I used to just hide away in my bed under the covers in my dark, dull room.

I locked myself away for days on end. Running away from normality. Apart from seeing my mum and dad, I would only come out of my room for doctors. I was very paranoid and sometimes suicidal.

My mind was racing for weeks and weeks. I was constantly drained, tired and only just wanted to sleep. I would hear voices and would think that people were out to get me.

The medication at the beginning was so strong it was designed to numb my brain and my mad, racing thoughts. After a good few months, the medication started to work and calm my racing thoughts down. I started to spend less time in my bed and room. I started to spend more time downstairs with my mum and dad.

Slowly I let family and close friends come to see me. But I was still very embarrassed to be diagnosed with a mental health condition. I wanted to keep it secret from as many people as possible and not let the outside world know what I was going through.

Eventually, after time I started to venture outside my home. First, I would go for small walks with my dad. In the beginning, I was very paranoid while walking. I felt like everyone was talking about me and needed my dad there to reassure me everything was ok.

My dad… he has been, over the years, my absolute rock. Whenever I've fallen ill in the twenty years that I've suffered with depression he has always been there to pick up the pieces. He has never turned his back on me no matter what I have done. He has been by my side one hundred per cent, all the way.

Even as a kid growing up he was always there for me. Was always there every Sunday without fail watching me play football. And nine times out of ten he would take me training or pick me up from training. Also, when I was doing my swimming three times a week he would be up outside the swimming pool with my mum waiting for me to train.

I had a great childhood. My dad made sure I never went without. I always had nice things for birthdays and Christmas. He always worked hard and provided for me and my mum. Without him, I don't know where we would have been, or what sort of life me and my mum would have had.

His mum and dad used to adore me and I used to love going round my grandparents' often on a Sunday for Sunday roast. They used to spoil me rotten. Especially at Christmas when we always used to go round Boxing Day. We were always down their caravan especially in the summer months when the football season was off. I have some great memories of being down that caravan with my mum, dad and his extended family, Such as aunts, uncles and cousins.

As I've gone on my journey of life my dad has been there every step of the way. He has been an absolute great dad to me, an amazing partner to my mum and the most brilliant grandad to my three children. My dad is my rock, but most importantly, my dad is my dad and my friend.

Then after a while, I started going on small walks by myself, I still had thoughts that people were constantly watching me and talking about me.

Slowly my walks became longer and my mind started to heal. My confidence really improving, I began to feel like my old self again.

Before My Depression

I had a great upbringing in Bermondsey. I went to a good primary school and had loads of friends. From a young age, I was taken to watch Millwall with my grandad. That's where my love for football began. Football was definitely my first love.

From the age of eight year's old, I played for and captained my local junior football team, Fisher. I had a great five to six years, playing for them. We were very successful and my team mates all got on so well. We were all very close friends on and off the pitch. Even though we were all of such a young age, we would all die for each other, during any match that we would play. We all had a winning mentality and there wasn't many games that we lost.

Life growing up on the estate was brilliant. Always something going on. If I weren't in the small square playing marbles, I was in the big square kicking a football or tennis ball up against the wall.

While on my first holiday abroad to America I learnt to swim and found my second love, swimming. I was so good I had England trials.

Primary school was great, I loved school and all my friends were amazing. I didn't go to the same secondary school as all my primary school friends. Nevertheless, I still liked and enjoyed my new school. I made loads of new friends and enjoyed my time there.

I started secondary school with a broken arm. As soon as I could get the plaster off, I was playing football for my year, the year above and two years above. In the second year, things started to really progress, I was picked to represent the district team (Blackheath).

I had to choose between my first two loves. Football or swimming. I loved and really enjoyed both. But to progress onto the next level I had to pick one or the other. I went with my first love… football.

I started to be even more successful now being a permanent fixture of the district team. I was also called up into the county (inner London) team on a regular basis. I even played a couple of games for Greater London.

My Sunday team, Fisher, were doing very well. Me and one of my best mates were given trials for Millwall, Charlton and Crystal Palace.

At the age of thirteen, we both signed for Charlton. We had to stop playing for Fisher. It was sad to leave our mates behind, but we had to do it as it was the next step forward.

Things on the pitch were going really well. Off the pitch, life was good too. I can't thank my mum, dad and grandad enough for all they did for me in my upbringing. I never went without. Always had new football boots on my feet when I needed them.

I liked school I saw it as more as a social thing than a learning environment. I always did enough but could probably have done more. I came away with decent exam results.

At the end of year ten, I was released by Charlton. I had trials for QPR, Coventry and Cambridge United.

Thankfully at the back end of year eleven, I was offered a YTS contract at Cambridge. So following my exams I moved sixty miles north to try to live the dream for the next two years.

How it all started:

I had two great years in Cambridge. At times — I'm not going to lie — I did find things tough up there but on the whole, the ups outweighed the lows.

At times I wasn't playing as much as I would have liked. But I just loved the routine of it. I liked that we all had our own little jobs to do on a day to day basis. Even cleaning the pros' boots on a cold winter's day was part of what really made me tick up there.

After the youth team manager got sacked in my second year, things started to go downhill. The new manager came in and he didn't really like me from the start. My playing time became less and less to the point where I wasn't starting and then not even getting on the pitch at all. I was training so well but I was just not liked. Towards the end of the second year, I was told that I wasn't being taken on for the third year.

My heart was broken. All the time, effort and dedication I had put in over so many years were just taken away from me in an instant. I was in pieces. So much so I was due to go on holiday with all the lads from football and really didn't want to go. I finally decided that I was to go along. I had a great time while we were away but the last day I lost the plot. I still can't remember to this day, what really happened to me on that last day. I only know what my best mate has told me. He said I was adamant I wasn't coming home, that I had nothing to come home for. In one way that was right… I had no football, no job to come home to. So I just didn't want to go home. My mates had to drag me to the airport and literally drag me onto the plane. I don't remember the journey home.

The next thing I really remember is being in my bedroom

at home, feeling like a sack of shit wanting my life to end. I just didn't want to be here anymore. That's when I knew I had a problem. But what was wrong with me still wasn't clear. I was so scared because I'd never ever felt like this before. What I now know is that this was my first breakdown.

Over the next nineteen years I would have a series of ups and downs. Some were really low times but nothing would prepare me for the massive high that I would have in April 2019.

I remember being with my first serious girlfriend. We were getting on so well that we decided to move in together. We had a nice one-bedroom flat above a shop in Chislehurst, where her mum used to work. I think I had a mild breakdown not long after moving in. It wasn't long before I was back to work. One day while at work I came over all funny and was very paranoid that everyone was talking about me and looking at me. That was it… I just didn't want to be here anymore. I remember the train journey home. I decided that this was it, that I would end my life as soon as I got home. I felt at peace within myself, knowing that I wouldn't be suffering any more. I finally got home. I felt calm. I wrote a note to my girlfriend and my mum, saying SORRY.

I then went to the kitchen drawer and took out a few sharp knives. I went upstairs to the bathroom and got undressed. I proceeded to stab myself all over my body as many times as I could before I passed out. The next thing I remember is being in the hospital toilet being cleaned up by my dad and grandad. I had to have an assessment at the hospital and then I was finally let home to my mum and dad's house where I was on suicide watch for quite some time. In time I split up with my girlfriend and I was up and down for a couple of years.

In 2002 I got together with an old friend from school. and in 2003 I went on to buy my first house. In July of the same year my son was born. Again I had ups and downs. I remember having a couple of very bad episodes where I had suicidal thoughts but I didn't try to do anything these times round. I split up with my son's mum when my son was around three or four. What followed was a very unstable part of my life.

Straight away I was looking to buy another property which I did about six months later. At the time I had a good well-paid job. My new house was just around the corner from where my son lived. But I was drinking a lot and even sometimes taking drugs (mainly cocaine). I was starting to rack up a bit of debt. I was for a couple of months paying my mortgage with my credit card.

This was the start of another really up-and-down time for me. My mental state started slipping and I very quickly became suicidal. This time I tried to end my life with an overdose. I was found by my girlfriend at the time who was ten years younger than me. I'm very thankful to this day to how she helped me and got me an ambulance. That got me to the hospital in no time.

I recovered pretty quickly from this episode and was back in my new house in no time. Things started becoming really rocky with me and my girlfriend. So much so I had a falling out with her dad. We had a massive row over the phone. I was so pissed off, I stormed round to his house to have it out with him.

He came charging out the house swinging at me with a baseball bat. I stumbled and fell over. He went back in and shut his door. I now had seen red and I don't care what happened, I was getting back into his house, to return the hiding he just gave me. So I took a run-up and tried to boot the door open, but to no avail — I just bounced off the door. There was a pushbike in the front garden, I decided to try and throw that through the window again, to no avail — it just rebounded off the window. I was getting in this house one way or another, if I liked it or not.

So I took another long run-up and tried to kick the door open. This time the door didn't open but I broke the wood panels on the door and went through into the hallway. He came at me and I chinned him, clean on the nose. He fell back onto the stairs and I jumped on top of him. My girlfriend's mum was hitting with the wood from the door. The next thing I knew I had two hands on my shoulders pulling me off saying, "You're nicked!" I was arrested and locked up in a police cell overnight. All charges were dropped but that was the end of me and her!

Saturday 6th April 2019

It all started on Saturday. Even though I hadn't had much sleep the previous week, I still was full of life and I was high as a kite. I was full of energy and laughter. I took my son to the cafe for breakfast. We had such a good time there. We were watching clips of *Only Fools and Horses*. We were laughing so much I had tears in my eyes and nearly fell off my chair. It seemed like we were in the cafe for ages as we had such a good time. I said to my son that in ten years' time I will have a red Ferrari.

Sunday 7th April 2019: I had a nice lay-in, the best night's sleep I've had in a very long, long time. I got up out of my pit and had bundles of energy. I had my breakfast and decided I was going to Gravesend to watch my son play football.

On the way there I decided to go to the sports shop as I wanted to buy a pair of boxing gloves for my cousins two-month-old baby. Every photo I had seen of him he has had his fist tightly clenched. I swear he's going to be a boxer, so I thought I'd get in early and buy him his first gloves. In permanent marker, I wrote W W D D (WHAT WOULD DARREN DO — and do the opposite) ONE SHOT (one punch and he's going to put you on your arse). I also brought a running vest for my cousin as I was adamant that she was going to run the London Marathon in a few weeks' time.

I got to my son's game nice and early, so I jumped in the car with my dad and we had a heart-to-heart chat about how I was feeling and my illness. He told me that needed to go to the doctor's in the morning. I agreed that's what I had to do. I told him I would go there first thing as soon as they open and wait to be seen.

I knew that I'd been slipping for quite some time. I had stupidly stopped taking my medication over 3 months ago. Slowly over those three months I started going downhill. Up until the end of March, when my world started to speed up. My energy levels started to increase to the point I didn't feel tired and didn't need to sleep. It felt like I was on drugs. I was up until four in the morning working in my garden, then up by seven a.m. to get my daughters ready for school as my wife was away for the week. As the week went on, I was having less and less sleep, but the more energy I had. My mind was thinking things at two hundred miles per hour and I felt so good within myself. The feelgood factor I had felt amazing and have never witnessed anything like this before. I felt a million dollars, I felt brand new and so happy. The happiest I've felt in years.

We got out of the motor and walked over to the side of the pitch. The game kicked off and I remember my son's team being three-nil up within the first ten minutes. What a great start. I am always quite vocal as a parent watching where I encourage the lads as much as I can and praise them when they do something right. But this particular day I was very loud. I could feel myself doing it, I was getting louder and louder but I just couldn't stop doing it. Again I just had so much positive energy. My dad told me to shut up and be quiet about ten times throughout the game. But I just wouldn't shut up. I really enjoyed the match. Felt like the best match I had watched in a long while.

My son came in the van with me and we were on our way to my mum and dad's for Sunday dinner. I was buzzing in the van full of praise to how well my son and his team had played. We were heading back to the A2. As I got closer to the motorway I noticed NEALLS CAFE had been demolished. It really threw me and I entered the A2 going the wrong direction, towards the coast. From that moment in time, I don't actually remember driving my van. So the next thirty minutes I completely blacked out. I half gained control on the south circular road as you do a left up to Grove Park station. I still wasn't fully in control. I reckon my grandad (who has been dead a few years now, who was a lorry driver) helped me drive my van safely. Autopilot took over but now I didn't feel in control, so I knew I needed to stop the van before I ended up crashing it. Eventually, I pulled into a quiet side road and brought the van to a halt. My head felt like it was going to explode. I quickly jumped out of the van and got some fresh air. As soon as I did it was like a pin had popped a balloon in my head and the pressure had been released. I walked to the end of the road, took a deep breath, counted to ten, took another deep breath and turned back towards the van and gave my son the thumbs-up.

I went back to the van to make sure my son was ok. He said in all the time I had driven him about he had never been scared with my driving, but he said he was scared stiff with what we had just been through. I went for a couple more laps of the pavement taking deep breaths to really clear my head. I got back to the van and felt as calm as anything. I felt absolutely fine now and drove to my mum and dad's.

We had a lovely dinner. Then I decided not to drive home and leave my van there. My dad dropped me home and I turned the heating on full blast, put my pyjamas on, and got myself an early night.

Monday 8th April 2019: I woke up at a decent time sweating my cods off to missed calls from my grandad. He had come over early and got to my doctor's as soon as they opened and got me an appointment for three p.m. I just got out the shower and I heard the door go. It was my grandad making sure I was okay. My mind had stopped racing and I felt really calm. But the feelgood Factor, still felt amazing and I was walking on cloud nine. Didn't have a care in the world. Everything was rosy.

(My grandad is the best grandad in the whole wide world. At eighty years old and he's still working on the river like he's been doing for sixty-five years since he was only fifteen. He's still strong as an ox. He has massive sausage-finger hands. One of his fingers is like two of mine.

He is always on the hurry-up in everything he does. He is like a whirlwind, but he is our whirlwind. He is so kind and has a heart of gold. Always the first person to help someone in need, always the first person to offer someone a lift to where ever they need to go.

I lived with my grandad from the day I was born. He has been like a father figure to me all my life. From a young age, I always remember being with him especially on a Saturday to give my mum a break. I remember him taking me to Asda most Saturday mornings and the only reason I liked going was that he used to buy me a small box of Lego. I couldn't wait to get home and open it to build it. Then most Saturday afternoons he used to take me to a football match. Mainly Millwall one week then Charlton the next. I was brought up the old school way of a docker just the way my grandad did, alternating between Millwall and Charlton just so all the lads could go on the beer together.

Saturday afternoons always consisted of going to football. He used to take me to Tottenham to watch Gazza every now and again. We also went to Chelsea quite a bit like a young boy as my granddad's brother was friends with the directors at Chelsea. Sometimes I was allowed to go up there and I always remember I loved to see the Chelsea pensioners. I respected them because they fought in the war.

My grandad encouraged me from a young age to play football. He took me to my first ever training session with Fisher behind their ground on Salter Road. There weren't many games of football I played in at Fisher and Charlton that he wasn't at. I always remember playing in a tournament near Peckham, he was working and got hit on the head. Blood everywhere but he still came to see how I and the team got on before he went to the hospital to get checked out. There was one game where he jumped over a tall fence to get the ball back. He was covered in anti-climb paint. Then we realised that there was a gate further down that was unlocked that he could have gone through. Again he was in a rush to get that ball back so we could carry on the game.

His life consisted of work, football and going to the pub. There wasn't a day he didn't go for a drink in the pub. Everybody loved him in any pub he used to go in. I remember the Red Lion is the one he went in most of the time. He was in there one night and they were all playing killer on the pool table. It was my grandad's go. He took the cue and hit the red which potted the white, he is colour blind so he sees no wrong in what he had just done, but the rest of the lads were on the floor pissing themselves laughing.

Another time he went out on the drink after giving blood, he was so drunk he could hardly walk and he fell down a manhole and cut all his head and face open. He had to go to the hospital.

My grandad has a great sense of humour. He is always the centre of a joke or taking the mickey out of you. He's an absolute wind-up. The only thing he gets muddled up with is names. If he calls you your name the first time you have had a result. Mainly he calls everyone Rod, even women. You do have a laugh a minute when you are around him and there's never a dull moment, always an old funny story being told.

I lay on the sofa, in my Millwall towel and just chilled out for a couple of hours. I then phoned my cousin and chewed her ear off for a couple of hours on the phone. I was talking to her about football and the hierarchy of our family. At the top of the hierarchy triangle was Nanny Bet, then everyone else was below her in generation order, right down to baby Jesse, who is the youngest. In my life just outside the hierarchy triangle was my old first team manager (Gaffer — Roy McFarland) and my old youth team manager (David Batch). Plus my best mate and my close pals.

I spoke to my cousin in detail about the England football team. About how I wanted to play for England and what tactics I would play. I was saying it as if I was the captain of the England team, wearing the three lions on my shirt and wearing the captain's arm band. I went through and picked my starting eleven:

* In goal — Jordan Pickford
* Right back — Kieran Trippier
* Left back — Ben Chilwell
* Centre half — Me

* Centre half — Harry Maguire
* Right wing — Jadon Sancho
* Left wing — Raheem Sterling
* Centre mid — Harry Winks
* Centre mid — Ross Barkley
* Striker — Harry Kane
* Striker — Jamie Vardy

I spoke to every one of my team mates in the changing room beforehand and told them what I expected from them for the game. Told them they needed to play with their hearts on their sleeves. As I say I was on the phone to my cousin standing at my back door, drawing out tactics with my finger on my glass sliding doors. I was adamant I was going to be leading the England team out at Wembley.

After coming off the phone to my cousin I phoned up a Ferrari dealership in South Kensington. I was trying to get a car for my son. The salesman said he had fifteen cars in his showroom and I said, "I'll have the lot."

GT1 812 SUPERFAST (that is worth £320,000)

With the number plate = GH 09 COX

G = GEORGE H = HARRY

0 = ZERO

9 = NUMBER 9 (MY SON'S SHIRT NUMBER) COX = SURNAME

I asked for the Ferrari to be delivered to my address any time before the 30th July 2020 which is my son's seventeenth birthday.

I was then on the phone to my old apprentice. He was asking advice about a fuse board he was replacing. He wanted to put a new surface-mounted fuse board over an old flush one and he was questioning what the best way of doing it was.

While I was on the phone to him I was doodling and this is what I wrote:

* Number 4 — my lucky number
* My doctor's appointment was at 3 p.m.
* Number 3 — this is a good number
* Horse number 3 won the grand national on Saturday
* I didn't even know that the race had taken place on Saturday
* Number 3 won
* 1st = 3 — Tiger Roll, 2nd = 18 — Magic Light, 3rd = 13 — Rathvinden, 4th = 36 — Walk in the Mill
* If I'd known, I would of had walk in the mill, because of Millwall
* I am a compulsive gambler
* And I really hate betting on horse racing
* The horses are NOT the problem. It's the idiots betting on them that's the problem
* Horse racing is a sport

Me the Gambler:

Up to January of this year, I was deep in trouble gambling my life away. The urges I was getting to have a bet were so powerful. There wasn't a minute of each day that went by that I didn't think about it. I was obsessed with doing it. I couldn't wait, to get in the casino (to play roulette) or into the bookies (to play the slot machines) or to play online (to play live roulette / online slots).

I can't really remember when gambling first became a problem for me. But what I do know, is that the last four years prior to January 2019, there probably weren't many days that I didn't have a bet or do one form of gambling. I used to wake up thinking about it, go to bed thinking about it and even sometimes have dreams about it.

The CASINO

The problem I had with gambling in the casino is that I really like the environment. I enjoyed going to and spending time there. If things were going well, I could spend the majority of the day there, no problem. I used to go in with X amount of money, normally around 200 pounds, and when that was gone it was gone. Whatever chips I would have won I would cash in. At times I won some big amounts of money. But that's what was dangerous. I knew if I was lucky enough that I had the potential to win large amounts of money. The thrill of winning was great. There was no better feeling than spinning that wheel, watching the little white ball fly around and it landing on your number. Be it thirty-six pounds or 360 pounds, a win was a win and it always felt good regardless the amount. Out of the three gambling platforms that I used to do, this one is one I really miss the most. I miss the interaction with people. I miss winning. I miss the whole casino environment. I had a good little system on the go, that I thought was quite successful and enjoyable. I always played the same numbers.

The BOOKIES

This was more of a quick fix on my way home from work when I had half an hour to an hour to spare. Again I would take out X amount to play with and once that was gone I would walk away. I would never bet on the horses or the dogs. I see them both as a sport. I used to play the slot machines most had a jackpot of 500 pounds. At times it could be a quick fix of winning a lot of money in a short space of time. Other times it could be a quick way of losing a lot of money. At times I was very successful and other times I wouldn't win a bean. The machines are very addictive. The hardest thing was walking away while you were up. It is so easy to put it back in again and lose the bloody lot.

ONLINE
For me this was the worst one out the lot. I could quite easily spend hundreds of pounds sitting watching the football scores come in while playing online slots. They are so addictive and you're not playing with real money. Feels like monopoly money. You can't physically see it going and coming into your hand. I started a new job two years ago that incorporates a shift pattern and quite a few night shifts. The night shifts were a killer. When I was bored, I just couldn't stay off my phone. It was so draining. One minute I'd won hundreds and sometimes thousands, the next minute I was down to my last twenty quid. Then back up again. It was like a money roller coaster, so many ups and downs. I've banned myself from all online gambling sites and I never want to go on an online site ever again.

Unfortunately, my depression brought on my gambling addiction. I wasn't born a gambler, it's something that's come on in my adult life. The gambling doesn't just cause a financial strain. It causes pain and hurt to everyone in your life. Gambling turns you into a liar. I wasn't brought up to lie.

I lied to friends and family on a number of occasions. Lying to get out of a lie, then forgetting what lies I was lying about. Asking to borrow money and lying about what it's for.

I haven't gambled for nine months, which I am so pleased about, and the last few months I haven't had the urge to gamble which is great. Long may it continue and long may I continue building bridges with my friends and family.

While I was getting myself ready and dressed to go to my doctor's I set up a Twitter account.

I set it up asking if anyone had seen Gazza and if they had to get in contact with me, as I wanted him to go play football with my son and me.

On my way to the Doctor's

I packed a big bag to go to son's football trial at Maidstone, where I thought Gazza would be as a guest appearance. I was adamant that Gazza (my boyhood hero) would be playing in the same game as my son. I was hoping to get down there in time to have a kick about with him, myself.

Inside the big bag I packed was:
* Two pairs of football boots
* Pair of Millwall shorts (orange ones)
* England shirt (with COXY number four on the back)
* Pair of football socks
* Towel
* Woolly and Tig toy (my youngest daughter's toy)
* Jess Glynne framed picture (my eldest daughter's picture)
* Gazza framed picture
* Millwall framed picture
* My white trainers

On the way to my doctor's I went to the shop and bought some bits to take with me to my son's football. I brought:
* A bottle of water
* Couple of fruit shoot drinks
* Bunch of bananas
* A seven-pack box of small Jaffa cakes biscuits
* Four pack of Snickers
* Packet of cigarettes for my nan

*   Bottle of Bells scotch for my nan

When I got to the doctor's I was late for my appointment so I had to wait in the waiting room to see the doctor. While I was in the waiting room I was having a laugh and joke with the children waiting to see the doctor. I was messing about with them, offering them drinks, sweets and fruit. I was playing a funny game with them and was taking the mickey out of them. One little girl I remember had chicken pox and was covered in spots. We were having a joke about her spots, I kept saying stay away as I don't want to catch them. Luckily her mum found me funny and wasn't offended by me or thought I was a weirdo. The girl's older brother kept on trying to take more sweets from me. He was laughing at why I had such a big bunch of bananas. Everyone in the waiting room were laughing with me, and I was in such a good mood. I could have sat there all day watching the world go by, watching patients come and go, having a laugh and joke with all the kids.

Every time I went to the toilet I took my Adidas Copa Mundial football boots with me. I left my big bag in the waiting room. But no way was I going to lose my football boots when I thought I was heading down to my son's game to play football with Gazza. I sat in the waiting room for two hours to be seen. But it didn't feel that long as I was having such a good time sitting there, watching the world go by.

Every so often I would go outside and be on the telephone to who I thought was my uncle or my cousin. I was also texting my cousins and my son with one word per text message at a time. I was writing one word then pressing send. I must have sent them hundreds of messages each. I must have been driving them mad.

While I was outside a car pulled into the car park with a black man driving with OLA on the personalised number plate. I was sure the man driving the car was my good friend Ola from secondary school and I thought he had be sent to me by my uncle to take me to my son's football game.

Finally, after waiting for a couple of hours, I got to see the doctor. I remember going into his room. But I can't remember a word that was said while I was in there. Apparently, the doctor ended my appointment by saying he was ordering me an ambulance. I didn't hear this and took myself outside with my big bag. After I came out I did a lap of the block. It was like I was being told in my head what to do by my uncle and my cousin. It felt like they were controlling my movements and where I was going. They made me do a second lap of the block, all the while I was hoping they were leading me to one of their cars and were going to pick me up and take me down to my son's football match. I thought I was then told to get on a bus home, which I did. The bus journey felt really quick like it was being driven at a hundred miles per hour. I got off the bus and walked up the road that led to my house. Halfway down the street a voice in my head told me to leave my big bag behind a car on some woman's drive. I left the bag there and took out my Adidas boots and continued with my walk home.

The next thing I know, is that I am sitting on my doorstep and my mum, dad and son turn up. They open the door and get me into the house and immediately phone for an ambulance.

IN MY HOUSE

I kept on saying, "IF MY NAN SAY YOU CAN, THEN YOU CAN."

* The police turned up straight away

* I thought my cousin, whose birthday it was today, who was at the *Only Fools and Horses* theatre production celebrating, was going to come on stage and everyone would sing *Happy Birthday* to him. I also thought that Gazza was going to turn up on stage, holding my cousin's nephew wearing the boxing gloves that I brought him and Gazza would jokingly punch my cousin on the nose. And present him with a big thirtieth birthday card from me.

* I also thought my other cousin was going to pull onto my drive any moment in my son's Ferrari, with Gazza sitting on the roof with her baby in the car seat in the front next to her.

* whilst sitting on the sofa I took my watch off and was playing with it a lot. twisting it forward then twisting in back.

* I had five -fifty-pence piece coins in my hand. I was constantly putting them in my football boot then taking them out again. Once they were out of my boot, I would put them in formation as you would see a number five on a dice. Then I would take them off the arm of the chair and put them back into my football boot.

* I was playing a game with the policeman, asking him how many coins I had in my hands. If he said four, I would say number five. If he said five, then I would say number four, and

so on and so forth. I could see I was really winding him up so I told: "who the F are you" and "get out my house". BUT if my nan says you can stay, then you can stay. So I let him stay.

    *   My dad wanted to use the loo and I said he couldn't. BUT if my nan says you can go for a wee, then you can go for a wee. So I let him use the toilet.

    *   I remember speaking to my friend on the phone and he was just saying listen to what everyone is saying to you and seek their help, that everything will be ok.

    *   I remember my son's mother turning up to pick my son up and telling her to look after him.

    *   I then sat back down on the sofa near the TV and thought Gazza was going to come on the television at Wembley stadium driving the Ferrari singing *Happy Birthday* to my cousin, with my cousin's face being beamed on to the big screen in the stadium. With all my family in the stands watching him.

    *   I remember two nurses turning up to check up on me, but I was doing no harm to myself or anyone.

    *   I had my Adidas Copa Mundial football boots with me throughout. Everywhere in the house I would go, I would take them with me. I wouldn't let them go. My dad had to hide them from me so I would leave the house!

    *   I finally left the house around one a.m. the following morning of my own accord and got into the police car. The policemen drove me to A & E.

WHILE IN A & E

I finally see someone at about two a.m. I think the nurse we saw could tell how ill I was so they quickly arranged for me to go into a private room away from the main A & E department. I was in there with my mum and dad. My mum and I were sitting on a sofa and my dad were sitting on a chair to the left of us.

For some reason I thought I owned the rights to *Only Fools and Horses,* so I kept dancing round the room singing the theme tune. Every time I sang it, I thought I was receiving money. I also thought that every time someone in the world sang it or watch an episode that I was receiving money also.

I also thought that every time someone in the world said four or five I received money as well. Four was my lucky number and five was my cousin's. Golfers were my best friends!

As it was my cousins thirtieth birthday I went out into the main A & E department and made everyone sing *Happy Birthday* to him. If they weren't joining in I was getting very angry and have a go at them, demanding they joined in with the singing.

For some reason I tried to run out of the room and out of the ward. My mum chased me (even though she was told if I run to let me go as there were police waiting outside for me). I got halfway out the ward, stopped, turned round and gave my mum a big cuddle. I told her I LOVED HER. We went back into the side room.

My dad was dying to use the loo but I wouldn't let him out of the room. Eventually my mum distracted me so he could get out the door. I didn't like the thought of him not being in the room with me. I felt safe having both parents in the room with me. Knowing I wasn't alone felt important, because deep down I was starting to feel scared. My mind was racing and my heart was pounding. It was going ten to the dozen. I could feel my heart beating through my chest. My mum and dad said they could see my heart through my shirt, as if it was going to burst. The nurses were worried I was going to have a heart attack.

While inside the room I noticed a plastic dado rail going around the centre of the room. I happen to knock it by mistake and it made a loud noise, like an alarm going off and started flashing red. I was dancing around the room pressing the buzzer setting the alarm off singing, *four four, five five, four five, five four*!! Again, mine and my cousin's lucky numbers. I was also trying to play the *Only Fools and Horses* theme tune by tapping the alarm and making it flash red.

My mum and dad got so annoyed with me dancing around pressing the alarm that they told me to, *Shut the fuck up!*

The nurses had to send for an electrician to isolate it and turn it off.

I remember having to keep five cups of water in the room with me. Every time someone came in the room, either nurses or security staff, I had to have five cups in the room. If there weren't then I would make that person go to the water machine and get some. It couldn't be four, it had to be five.

The next thing I remember is my great auntie randomly turning up in the A & E department with one of her friends. She said she heard me singing from outside the room I was in.

She could recognise my voice as I was singing again. She came into to see us. I said she smelt of my nan — like cooking or fags or something. I told my aunt that I really liked her body warmer that she was wearing. I said to her that I wanted it and gave her my wallet in exchange for it. I gave her a big kiss and massive cuddle. I then started to dance around the room again like a lunatic singing the *Only Fools and Horses* theme tune again. My aunt was really laughing at me. She found what I was doing so comical and was singing along with me. She never did give me her body warmer. Then my aunt left the room.

In her place I remember one of the security guards coming in. He was sitting there chatting with my dad. He was a big strong man, a lot bigger than me. I didn't like what he was saying so I confronted him, then grabbed him and then tried to hit him. There was a little scuffle between us both and then we got pulled apart. I told him he was an idiot and he left my room.

Then the police came into my room. One was a tall black policeman and one small gorgeous-looking policewoman. As soon as I see them both I liked what I see. Both of them were really friendly and helpful. I gave the policeman a big cuddle. We spoke loads about football and where he grew up. He was kind enough to keep getting me cups of water, remembering it was five cups to be in the room at any one time. We spoke for quite a while and were having a right laugh.

I played a drawing game with the policewoman and said I would buy her any car that she wanted but only if she would handcuff me. She said she wanted a pink Range Rover. I was having a right good laugh with them both. They both made feel really safe and calm. The policewoman was tiny but she had lovely eyes. I promised her I would get her the car she wanted if she looked after me and kept me safe. Also, she would have to handcuff me to get me into the ambulance, and she did.

So I finally left the A & E department in a special ambulance. With two ambulance crew. The policeman came inside with me and the policewoman followed behind in the police car. While I was in the ambulance I got talking to the policeman, I really liked him. I told him he could have the Ferrari that I got for my son, as I ordered the wrong number plate for it. I told him to get the keys from my son and that I give him permission to go collect it and drive it off my driveway the next morning. We had a really good chat in the ambulance and we were getting on like a house on fire. We were talking about football a lot. He said he was a Liverpool fan but said he had never been to a game. So I offered to take him to a game very soon. He said he would really like that. We also spoke about watching England. We discussed what was the best current team.

I was adamant we were heading to Maidstone, to watch or play football with my son who had a game down there. I told the policeman that we would be meeting Gazza as well, as he would be at the ground waiting to play football with us. I could see out the window that we were on the M20 heading down towards Kent. We finally pulled up at our location. As they got me out the ambulance the policewoman was there ready and waiting for me. I begged her to handcuff me again and take me into the ground as I said it would be funny and everyone would piss themselves laughing including Gazza.

The 'ground' as I thought was Maidstone United, was in fact Maidstone mental health hospital. But I now thought I was going out onto a pitch to play football for England's national team, wearing the three lions on my shirt. I was rushed from the ambulance with the police into a waiting room that I thought was behind the football changing rooms.

In Maidstone Mental Health Hospital

For some reason, while I was in this waiting room an old football friend of mine called Jay Lloyd Samuel came to my mind.

Jay Lloyd unfortunately had died about a year earlier — I remember the day I heard he had died. I was driving through central London and heard the tragic news on the radio. I pulled over and stopped my van. I wiped a tear away from my eye and took a moment to digest the sad news I had just heard. I noticed a black tramp sitting with his back against a wall, begging for money. I continued with my day but just couldn't get it out of my head. When I got home my wife knew there was something up and asked me what was wrong. I told her an old football pal of mine, who I used to play with as a kid, was in a car crash after dropping his kids off to school and had died. My wife and I agreed that life was too short. I just couldn't believe he had gone, it really hurt me.

I was sitting in this circular waiting room with windows all around with the policeman who I now thought was Jay Lloyd's brother. We had a conversation about Jay Lloyd. We both were getting upset. I said, "You miss him, don't you?" and he nodded. I was still thinking I was going out to play football for England. I told the policeman that I was going to play this game for Jay Lloyd and make him proud. I was wearing a smart long-sleeved grey polo shirt with a black button-down collar. I took my shirt off. I found a tube of toothpaste in my coat pocket. I turned my shirt over and lay it flat. On the back of it, in toothpaste, I drew a number four for my lucky number and drew a number eight for Jay Lloyds number, making a forty-eight. I let the tooth paste dry for a bit. Then put the shirt back on. Rolling up my sleeves, I was getting ready to go play the game of my life.

I took my jeans off. I was now down to my pants, my grey long-sleeved shirt and my suede Chelsea boots on (they were going to be my football boots for the game). I was ready to go out on that pitch and play one last game for England and the three lions.

Inside the circular waiting room there was a wall of windows. Behind the windows is an office with people in (I now know that these people were doctors and nurses), but at the time I thought that the people in the office were Jay Lloyd's family. I had a massive bruise on my left thigh, which I got from A & E — they had to fight with me to get the medication inside me. I thought every time I touched my bruise that Jay Lloyd's family received money. They could see on the computer screens in the office that money was going into their accounts. Even though the bruise was very sore and painful to touch, I held my hand firmly on it and keep my hand on it constantly for as long as I could bear. I thought the harder I pressed the bruise, the more money the whole family were receiving!

I finally got let into the corridor that ran alongside the office. I thought the corridor was the tunnel to go out onto the pitch. Waiting for me, which I now know, were a couple of male doctors. But at the time I thought one was Jay Lloyd's father and the other I thought was Jay Lloyd's brother. For some reason I took my shirt off, I folded it up and gave it to his father. I took my boots off and gave them to his brother. I did both of these as a gesture of respect of their late, great son.

I'm now down to my pants and just a captain's armband. Ready and waiting to take the field to go out to war, by playing football and winning the battle. I was non-stop pacing up and down the tunnel (the corridor), waiting for the referee to say it was time to call us out onto the pitch. There were loads of rooms located off both sides of the tunnel. In the last room I looked in was a tramp, a black tramp. The same tramp I saw on the day when I found out about Jay Lloyd being dead, that I heard on the radio in the work van up central London.

The tramp inside the room was sitting on the floor with his back against the wall with his knees up to his chest. I tapped on the door window to get his attention. He stood up and came straight up to the window. I knew straight away that this tramp was Jay Lloyd. It made me very angry and sad that this tramp stood on the other side of the door was him. I started running up and down the tunnel kicking and hitting the doors and walls shouting and screaming saying, "That's NOT JAY LLOYD, PLEASE TELL ME THAT WAS NOT JAY LLOYD!" But it was! I was still in my pants, still pressing my bruise, giving his family more money. I was crying and getting myself in a right old state as I could see how much of a mess he was in.

I told Jay Lloyd to strip down to his pants like me and get out here. I wanted him to come play football with me for the three lions one last time, like we used to do when we were kids. He was a great player, hard as nails. I consistently had my hand pressing on my left thigh. It bloody hurt but I didn't care because I thought Jay Lloyd's family were getting more and more money, every time I touched it.

The next thing I remember is being outside and it was dark, with his father (a mental health doctor) putting me into the back of a caged police van.

In the Police van

I was put in the back of a caged police van. The only thing inside was a bottle of water. I remember it being dark outside. Inside the back of the van were two police officers that I believed was my good friend from school Ola's father and uncle. They are two older black men. I don't remember an awful lot of the journey in the police van, but what I do remember, is that we were talking about years of evolution-the current times in England to old times in Africa. I remember Ol's father telling me a story of how he had to walk miles to get clean water for his family, whereas nowadays he can just get it from a tap. He also mentioned about chasing elephants. They kept passing bottles of water through the hatch in the grill to me. The next thing I remember is being in a lobby area with Ola and few other black friends of mine from football (they turned out to be nurses from a mental health ward). The lobby I now know is that of a mental health hospital in Dartford, called LITTLE BROOKE.

First Time in Little Brooke hospital

I ended up in the reception area lobby with who I thought was Ola and three other black blokes. Ola was very smartly dressed wearing a grandad cap. As soon as I see him I gave him a big bear hug of a cuddle. I thanked him for helping me at me doctor's when his car pulled into the car park and thanked him for getting his father in helping me get me here in the police van.

We spoke a lot about football. He was winding me up saying he was a West Ham fan and that he now lives in Scotland (Glasgow). He said he now goes to watch Rangers quite a lot at Ibrox. He asked if I was still a Millwall fan and I said yes. He remembered the time when I took him to his first live football match as teenager down to the Den to watch Millwall versus Liverpool. He said he loved the atmosphere down there and he could never forget the roar of the Millwall crowd. He said there is nothing in football like it. And he is right, you can't beat a packed Den for the electric atmosphere.

The next thing I knew, was that another one of my very good friends called Jason appeared out of a side room that I was adamant that Gazza was inside. I was getting all happy I was finally going to meet my boyhood hero. Gazza had been my ideal for years, since I was little and could remember first watching football. My grandad used to take me over to Tottenham to watch him. I loved everything he did and worshipped the ground he walked on.

My good friend Jason looked so old, it was like I went way too far forward in time and everyone now looked very old, at deaths door. Jason spoke to me very calmly and said everything was going to be okay. He also said that everyone here, was here to help me get better.

Hearing Jason suggest I wasn't well gave me the hump and I completely lost the plot. I went for Jason and grabbed him by the throat because I didn't believe I was ill and he thought I was ill. It took four male members of staff to pin me down. I thought I was being mugged and/or attacked at this moment in time. It felt like I was having a knife go into my bum and I thought I was being stabbed (which turned out that I know now that it was the big needles going into my bum for medication). I managed to fight off the four blokes that were holding me down, and while I lost the plot, amongst all the commotion I locked about ten doctors and nurses in their office. I was finally restrained and because I kicked off I was drugged up to the eyeballs, and put in ISOLATION for the night!

Night in isolation
After my night in isolation, I wake up laying on a blue rubber mattress on the floor in just my pants and my grey long-sleeved shirt with forty-eight still in toothpaste on the back. I feel like I've had the best night's sleep ever and I feel like I have been asleep for ages.

In the room was:
* Me
* Blue rubber mattress
* External window with grill
* Exit door

* 2 x internal windows with shutters
* Toilet

I felt at peace, all alone by myself but I felt very content, I felt at ease and the calmest I had felt in years.

The next thing I remember is getting a thought of my first serious girlfriend's father, who was a massive Glasgow Rangers fan. I also now know that unfortunately due to illness he was now forced to live his life from a wheelchair. I was adamant that he was waiting outside the isolation room ready to greet me. So I thought to myself I need to give him something. But I had nothing to give. Apart from the shirt on my back. So I took my top off folded it nicely how a footballer would want it with the number 48 facing upwards. I waited at the door holding the shirt ready to present to my ex's father in his wheelchair.

The next thing I remember is being bundled out of police van/ambulance vehicle and being met by loads of staff in a building I thought was a royal hospital. I was moved into a lobby where I stood at the bottom of a flight of stairs. I now know this was a holding hospital called Roehampton.

Roehampton Hospital

I was now transferred to Roehampton hospital. This is where I had loads of weird and wacky thoughts. I can only put them down to dreams, as every time my mother or a family member called to check on me they always said I was sound asleep.

I first remember getting out of some sort of police van or ambulance vehicle. I was greeted by a sea of people (that I can only think now were doctors or nurses). They led me into a lobby area that came to a set of stairs. I remember a posh female talking to me at this point saying they must take me up the stairs. She said once we were up there they would give me tea and biscuits.

At this moment in time I thought I was a lion and that at the top of the stairs was a room which had Her Majesty the Queen in it!

I was roaring like a lion and the doctors struggled to get me up the stairs, one step at a time. Being a lion I thought I was there to defend the Queen. But I wasn't allowed to go into the room to see her. They finally got me the lion to the top of the stairs. We went through a set of secure double doors and I was led into the first room on the left hand side. Inside the room it was a blue and red padded cell room. One minute the room was BLUE for Millwall the next minute the room was RED for Charlton. The floor was padded matting, the walls (left and right) were padded and on the back wall was a long deep padded seat/bed with padded pillow at either end of the

43

bed. As I say the colour of the pads within the room kept on changing colour from blue to red, then red to blue, changing quite quickly. Finally the colour stopped at blue for MILLWALL.

Next thing I know I was crouched down on my hands and knees pretending to be roaring lion who was there to protect the Queen. I kept saying and repeating three lions on the shirt and I was taking three fingers to my chest on the left hand side by my heart. Thinking the fingers symbolised the three lions on an England football shirt.

I next remember coming out of the padded room into a large circular room with a big TV by the window. Laying on big bean bags was a very young fat version of my cousin. He was watching football on the TV. Also in the room was my son's stepdad, who asked how my son was doing at football and if he was good enough to play for Arsenal.

I sat down on a chair on the right hand side of the room. A black man with dreadlocks came and sat next to me. He spoke to me in a strong Caribbean accent. I see him as a cross between my grandad, Ben, and his good black mate, Clive, from Saint Lucia. He told me that dinner would be served up soon and it would be my nan's Spanish spaghetti on the menu.

I next remember sitting at the dinner table and a lady putting a big bowl of food in front of me. I took a mouth full, it was the spiciest thing I have ever had — it nearly blew my brains out. Somehow I managed to finished it all. I washed it down with a couple of pints of orange juice.

I next remember a room at the back of the main room with its door open. I was led to believe that her royal harness the Queen was inside and that my nan was coming to meet her but I wasn't allowed to go in the room or meet the Queen. I had to wait outside and be the LION again protecting her. My nan came and she went into the room where the Queen was sitting. My nan was in there for what felt like ages while I waited outside guarding the door. The Queen and my nan had tea and cake together, plus a nice long chat. My nan came out with a massive smile on her face. She thanked me so much for making the meeting possible.

I next remember waking up in a very comfortable single bed within a hotel like bedroom. In the room was:

* A bed
* 3 x floor to ceiling skinny wardrobes (that looked like what you would have in a posh football changing room — like individual changing areas)
* A desk and chair
* A window looking out to a car park
* A door leading out to a corridor
* And lastly a picture hanging in the middle of the right hand wall.

The picture was of two boats — a RED one and a BLUE one. A red one for Charlton and a blue one for Millwall. The boats were moored up in a lovely little harbour just as the sun was setting. I was getting a strong message / feeling that the picture symbolised my grandad who has worked on the River Thames all his life as a waterman and lighterman from the age of fifteen years old.

I was playing some sort of counting game and I had my finger pressed against the picture moving from left to right then right to left but my finger always had to end on the blue boat for Millwall (as Millwall always beat Charlton).

I next remember waking up and looking out the window, thinking I was in Buckingham Palace, seeing down the Mall on the morning of the London Marathon day. (The best marathon in the whole world). I cheered all the runners on from my window as the race unfolded. After watching for hours I could finally see my cousin come round the corner and head towards the finish line. I went out onto the balcony of Buckingham Palace and give her a special wave and cheer.

I next remember being a "LEAP YEAR". Yes that's right a leap year and that my life was running parallel to a primary school female friend who turned out and went on to be a very successful women's professional football player. It was like I was playing out my life as her. Enjoying the highs of success and feeling her pain of her lows. Being a leap year like I thought we were that me and her would only have a birthday every four years. Not every year like any other normal person. So instead of being in our mid-thirties we were both only about nine years of age.

Time kept on jumping back to when we were little and at school together. We both went to the same primary and secondary schools. We spent a lot of time together growing up and we played loads of football with each other. She was better than most of the boys. The thought of being a leap year was very bizarre but it felt good and felt like we both had so much energy because we both still felt so young at heart. It ended up with me being as successful at football as she was, playing for decent clubs and playing many times for my country (England) in big tournaments.

I next remember being on the council estate where I grew up on playing out with all the other kids. We all used to play marbles on the drains in the small square or football in the big square or run outs on the estate opposite. Most nights I used to be out playing downstairs with my mates. There was nothing better than being allowed out after school to play. If no one was about to play I would go down and kick a football or tennis ball, up against the wall. My childhood was great on the estate and I fitted right in. Every Sunday without fail all my friends would be out and we would have a football match in the big square that seemed to last for hours. We would only stopped and call it a day once the light was so bad that you couldn't see the ball. Every year in April all the kids from the estate used to go with their parents to Jamaica Road to watch the London marathon pass by. We used to hold out cut up oranges and sweets for the runners the take out of our stretched out hands.

I next remember being outside Buckingham Palace pretending to be a lion protecting Her Majesty the Queen alone with four other lions. So five of us in total. We were all standing big and strong. Nothing and no one could get past us. I felt so much pride being there and protecting the Queen.

I next remember running up and down the corridor playing football with a tin can. I don't know who I was playing football with but we were playing a five aside game. We had a goal at each end of the corridor. At one end of the corridor was a glass window. Outside the window the sun was shining but the surroundings weren't England. It looked like somewhere abroad like the Dominican Republic. I could feel the intense heat coming through the window.

I next remember being locked away on my own in a toilet. The toilet decoration wise looked like a toilet at my work place. I could hear voices coming from the drain. I was sitting on the floor with the drain between my legs. The voices coming from the drain were getting louder and clearer. I could hear the voices of Bobby Moore, Geoff Hurst, Peter Shilton, Gary Lineker and Gazza. I was going to be there captain and I was going to lead them out at the old Wembley against a Liverpool legends team. I led the team out and with sang the national anthem. I loved having the three lions crest on my shirt. There was nothing better. We won the game three nil and Gazza scored a hat trick.

I then found myself back on the floor with a tennis ball in my hand and just like in the film *The Great Escape*, was throwing the ball up against the wall and catching it. It seemed like I was doing this for hours on end.

Still in the toilet, I started to drink the cocktail Harvey wall banger. I had drank so many I felt so drunk that I could hardly stand up straight. Then a random gorgeous lady appeared in the toilet with me. We were dancing the night away and getting down with our bad selves. We danced, and danced, and danced. And drank some more cocktails. I could see that the lady was stunning and had a great body but I couldn't actually see her face so I don't know who it was I was having a great time with. I was so drunk I was sick down the drain.

I next remember one of my old bosses being there with me. He had his own family-run business and all his family were here with him including his new wife that he only just got married to. His wife and his mum got locked in the blue padded room along with me. While inside the room his wife confessed to his mum that she had been having loads of affairs since they were together. His mum was fuming and very angry with her so we fed her to the lions outside. Her husband (my old boss) was so very grateful to me for getting rid of her, that he gave me two big bags of money.

I next remember looking out of my bedroom window and seeing my grandad drive into the car park. I could see out my window that he reversed into a space. Then another car pulled into the car park and it was my grandad's best mate. He parked up too on the other side of the car park. They both stayed in their cars as if they were waiting for me to come out and see them. They waited and waited there for ages.

I next remember looking out of my bedroom window and it was pitch black outside. I could hear and then see two mopeds that kept driving up and down outside the car park. Both riders were wearing big rucksacks on their back. They pulled away. As the lion I was, I followed them to the Houses of Parliament where they both planned to blow it up. On their back inside the rucksacks were two bombs. I managed to stop them blowing up the Houses of Parliament. They were both from the IRA.

Transferred to hospital in Dartford:
The next park of my long journey is very bleak and I don't remember much that went on. I now know that this is when I was very ill and at my worse. I arrived at Littlebrooke hospital in Dartford least not knowing how I got there or if I was even alive. I don't remember how I got there from Roehampton hospital. I now know this is when I was at my worse and treatment was allowed to start properly. I was getting the best possible treatment from the best health professionals. The early stages I was given a lot of injections to keep me calm and to stop my mind and my heart from racing. But for the first few weeks I don't remember a thing.

I still to this day don't know how long this was into my stay at Littlebrooke hospital, but I first remember fighting with four big doctors, who had to pin me down to give me my injections in my bum cheek. This went on which felt like a few days.

I kept ripping my clothes off. Ripping my T-shirts, shorts and pants into shreds. I remember having two nurses on my door twenty-four hours a day. They were there for my safety and looking out for me.

As I slowly got a bit better my family were allowed in to the hospital to come visit me. First my mum and dad, then my nan and then my great auntie.

I had a bad habit of splashing water from the sink in the bathroom over myself and face. I remember I kept getting told off for doing this.

I slowly become better and better and brighter and brighter. I started to keep my clothes on and stopped ripping them off. My head started becoming clearer and clearer as the drugs started to kick in and I was getting more used to the dosage.

I remember one time when my mum and nan came to visit me, that one of my favourite male nurses had made me a bowl of fruit salad. I squirted a big bit of squirtie cream just as I was tucking into that as my mum and Nan came into my room and I was so pleased to see them. I could feel I had turned a bit of a corner and my brain was starting to heal. My alertness was coming back and I started to feel half normal again.

One female nurse in there reminded me to look at of an ex-girlfriend of mine. When I first met her I was adamant it was her and kept calling her my ex's name. She took it in good heart and we got on really well. We always joked throughout my stay in there and I always called her my ex's name. This particular nurse always had a pink glittery pen. I loved her pen and I tried to nick it off her every day without fail. But she wouldn't let me have it. She said the only way she would let me have the pen if I brought a pair of pink glittery shoes and wore them for her. Thing is I think she knew if I could of I would of. I even told her to go buy me a pair when she was off and I'd wear them for a week. Anything for this poxy pen I really wanted it. But she stood firm and wouldn't let me have it.

I finally became well enough to have my own room. The room was very basic with:
* A bed with a blue mattress
* A triangle-shaped desk
* A very heavy chair
* A open shelf wardrobe
* A en-suite shower and toilet

Once I was in my own room I really started to enjoy the routine of what hospital life brought me: 8am was breakfast — porridge and toast

Twelve midday was lunch — soup, main meal and dessert five p.m. was dinner — soup, main meal and dessert ten p.m. was supper — toast.

In between meals there was a mixture of activities. Along with courtyard time where we were allowed to go outside for fresh air and a walk. Luckily most days the sun was shining so it was nice outside. Also we were allowed to go in the pool room where there was a computer which we were good to play music from YouTube. We used to take turns to pick a song.

Slowly I became better and better, stronger and stronger. By this time I had grown a big burly beard. I liked my beard. It was like my shield that I could hide behind. I felt safe.

I really started to make friends in there, not just with the patients but with the nurses as well. The nurses were fantastic with me, so loving, caring and thoughtful towards me. I had my favourites in there, but there wasn't one in there that I didn't like, even the cleaners used to talk to me on a daily basis. We had a good bunch of patients in there as well, everyone got on really well and we all looked out for each other.

I was issued with a section 17. Which meant for thirty minutes per day I could go with a nurse for a walk around the grounds of the hospital. I really looked forward to this every day. It used to break my day up.

I was lucky enough to always have a lot of visitors on a weekly basis. Every Thursday my great auntie used to come in and see me. She used to bring me in a big bottle of apple juice that she used to buy from her farm shop. We would sit there and drink it and call it our champagne. She came in at the same time every week, three p.m. One week she was late and I had a go at her. The reason why she was late was because she left home and had forgotten the apple juice. So she went back home to get it. We always had a laugh. It really gave me a lift seeing my auntie every week.

Every Saturday my mum and dad would come a visit me. They always brought me goodies in, like sweets and chocolate. They would stay beyond the two hours until they were virtually being thrown out. On the odd occasion my son was allowed to come in and see me. He would always take the mick out of my beard, laughing that it had loads of ginger and grey in it. It was lovely seeing my son. Near the end of my stay, I think it was the last weekend before I came out. I was allowed to take a section 17 at the same time as my son, my mum and my dad were there. Just seeing my son and giving him a big cuddle meant the world to me. I remember him showing me highlights on his phone of a football match him and my dad had been to the day before. Watching football for the first time in an age made me feel good and made the hairs on the back of my neck stand up.

Obviously, I missed my children while I was in hospital, but a close second, I missed the freedom of watching football as and when I liked.

On a Sunday my mum used to bring my nan in to see me. This used to be my best visit of the week. I adore my nan, she has been by my side every step of the way.

What can I say about my nan? Well, she was the first person to see me when I came into this world.

She has been 110 per cent by my side ever since. Thanks, Nan! She even paid to get me back from Scotland one time when I was stuck and had no money.

She is the most honest person I know and so trustworthy it's unbelievable. You can tell her anything in confidence and you know it won't go any further. Many a time I've confided in my nan and she always gives you her honest opinion.

She has stuck by me like glue all through my illness. Every step of the way she has been by my side. Giving me all the love and support that a grandchild needs and more. I can't thank my nan enough, for sitting with me and virtually babysitting me when I was at my lowest and when I was suicidal. Even just knowing she was downstairs made me feel safe. She used to come to my house and sit with me just so my mum and dad could go to work.

This time round when I was sectioned, every Sunday without fail while I was in hospital my nan used to come and visit me. She always came bearing gifts and treats. Even something as simple as a bag of apples. But every time I would have an apple I would think of my nan. She has been a massive part of my recovery since I've been home from hospital. Nearly every week I go round there and she feeds and waters me.

My nan is a great cook and she makes it look so easy. There's nothing like my nan's Spanish spaghetti and bacon rolls. I also love the fact she always has loads of ginger nut biscuits in the cupboard. My nan has always been a massive part of my life. Most weekends I used to spend at her house sleeping over.

In my eyes there is no one like my nan. I adore her so much. Words can't describe my love for her. There is no one in this world like my nan. Even at my wedding she was the only person on that dance floor all night long. She is a diva. And can she move when she gets going. I would do anything for my nan and help her, as much as I can.

Yes, she likes a fag and yes, she likes a scotch but she's my nan, and my nan can do whatever she wants, in my eyes.

My nan's husband… what a man he was. A very quiet man but a very loving and caring man. He would do anything for anyone. Especially family. He adored his family and was so good looking after all us kids as we were growing up.

He loved a baby. My son loved being around Ben. They were always so happy together. He was a very patient man always had time to help everyone. He taught nearly everyone in our family to drive.

He was a great driver himself and he loved his model cars and lorries. What a collection he had. My nan still has them in her living room, now.

One of my earliest memories of Ben was his vintage lorry that he had when I was a kid. He used to take it to car shows and I remember riding on the back of it. There was nothing like his red lorry. It was a close second for the love he had for my nan. He absolutely adored her. There was no one like my nan in his eyes.

He was a very strong man. I always remember him doing some sort of building work or DIY projects. He was a genius with his fancy writing and graphics. A really good drawer. There was nothing he couldn't turn his hand to.

At Christmas I remember there always being thousands of decorations and lights inside and outside the house.

He really enjoyed a nice drop of Jameson's and he liked nothing better than a nice Harvey Wallbanger cocktail, on a bright summer's day. He worshipped being in the sun and he was always a lovely golden colour. Always looked so healthy.

He used to take me to football training in Cambridge twice a week and he didn't really like football. You would never hear Ben swear, unless maybe, on the odd occasion when he had a drink. In the early stages of my depression when I self-harmed I remember Ben always being there for me and supporting me every step of the way.

To me Ben is a legend, and I miss him so much.

Close to the end of my stay in hospital, I was getting bored. But boredom was a good thing, which meant I was getting a lot better. I can't thank the nurses enough for looking after me and getting me well. The main nurse in the hospital was amazing, such a lovely lady. She managed in the end to get me released straight from that ward, which is very unheard of. You are not normally discharged home straight from my ward. You normally have to go to an open ward, stay there for a few weeks, then released fully from there.

I remember the day I was released from hospital like it was yesterday. It was Friday 31st May 2019. I was called into the ward round meeting in the morning to see the doctors. They told me the good news that I would be going home today and that my mum and dad were on their way up to pick me up. I can't describe how happy I felt. I couldn't believe I was going home. My mum and dad turned up, I packed up all my stuff, said my goodbyes to all the nurses and patients. Everyone wished me well and good luck. The first thing I wanted to do was go and see my nan.

When I first came out, the adrenaline was pumping through my body and I was walking on cloud nine. It was great to be out in the open.

It felt very strange being in a car. Even down to making a cup of tea felt really weird. The day after coming out I went to the barbers. I got my hair cut and had my beard shaved off. It felt so good. I finally felt like me again.

September 10th: is suicide prevention day. For anyone that has felt suicidal or who is feeling suicidal, I really do feel for you.

I have been there on more than one occasion and definitely have the T-shirt. A couple of times I tried to take my own life. Thankfully I wasn't successful and I'm here to tell the tale.

It can only be described as the worst possible feeling you can ever have. To be that low is scary and even think not being here is the best thing, then you can't be so far from the truth. The pain and hurt it leaves behind is unthinkable.

What parent wants to see their son or daughter die before them? To have to bury your own child I can only imagine must be the worst thing in the whole wide world. I'm so glad now I was unsuccessful! It would have ripped my family apart.

Since my last attempt, I have had very low points and I

have had further bad thoughts. But I now know these thoughts are not right. I won't let these thoughts beat me. I'm not the strongest person in the world by far, but what I have got is a massive heart and I will never give up.

I can talk about things now but when I first had depression and for years and years I was embarrassed by the stigma around mental health. I was frightened to talk and open up to people. So my message is open up and talk. A problem shared is a problem halved.

If you or you know someone who now today or in the future is having suicidal thoughts, then seek help and talk.

MY RECOVERY

Saturday 14th September 2019: My first Millwall away game of the season. In fact, it's my first away game since I can remember, been a while. Who would have thought I'd be able to take the six-hour coach trip up to Blackburn, back in April?

Six months ago, I was in a very dark place. The darkest place I have ever been in my whole life. My bipolar for the first time went manic. So manic my heart was racing so much I nearly had a cardiac arrest. I can only describe it as an absolute roller coaster of a ride.

If you took a piece of paper, turned it on its side, drew a line from left to right in the middle of the page (that line being normal). Then run your finger up from normal, as quick as you can to off the page, and keep going. well, that was me, in a place I had never been before. Well and truly off the page.

The last couple of days before I was sectioned I was so happy and had so much energy. If I could bottle up how I was feeling over this time I'm sure people would pay good money to sample this. But when I was first hospitalized things took a turn for the worse. I became quite aggressive to staff and wouldn't take my medication. It was taking four strong men to hold me down to sedate me.

But credit is due to all the nurses in the hospital who stuck by me at my lowest ever point in my life. In all my nineteen years of suffering from a mental health condition, I have never been sectioned. So the nurses pulled my life around. Without them, I wouldn't be here to tell the tale of my first away trip in many moons.

Even though we lost today it has been an amazing day for me. I have tried to strip myself back to the core. Tried to find me again. My first love was football. So I'm trying to keep things and do things, simple. So as the sun sets and as we edge closer to home I can take a lot of positives out of today, considering six months ago I was locked up on a mental health ward.

Tuesday 17th September 2019

I woke up today feeling not so good. Struggled to get out of bed. I was awake but had no motivation to get up.

I felt very alone and emotional this morning, but I just don't know why. Making my breakfast was a big effort, getting into the shower seemed hard work. Once I had washed I felt a bit more alert.

Thankfully I had something to look forward to, I was going to have lunch at my nan's. Walking round to the bus stop, I just didn't feel right and was shaky.

It just shows you how vulnerable we all can be and I still am. Six months ago I went through the worst experience in my life. Locked away for two months without seeing my kids, friends and loved ones. The four months since my release from hospital it has been a very slow road to recovery. I'm not far away from being back to my best.

Someone asked at the weekend how I was feeling, I replied, "I haven't felt this good in years!" Then I wake up today and don't feel too great. It's a massive rain check which has made me realise a few things. Least, not the thing that I am and always will be at my most vulnerable when I feel better.

Today has been a lesson learnt that I can never be complacent and always need to be on top of my game. I can't let things slip. If I let slip things can very quickly go backwards. I'm glad I woke up how I did this morning. It's no coincidence, that going to my nan's has cheered me. I'm so lucky to have such supportive family and friends.

THANKS MUM

Saturday 30th November 2019: So today my mum took me up the Shard for my birthday. What can I say about my mum? She is my rock!

Everyone knows how much of a bad year I've had with my mental health, what with being sectioned for two months. My mum has been there every step of the way. She has always been there to pick up the pieces when I've been at my lowest. There is no one like my mum, she means the world to me. What I have put her through over the years, but she has stuck by me through thick and thin. Always there to pick me up and dust me off and go again. There wasn't a day going by in that hospital, that my mum wouldn't phone to see how I was doing. Even at the beginning when I was very ill and couldn't come to the phone, I know now she was calling three times a day.

Every weekend without fail she would come and visit me. On a Saturday with my dad and then on a Sunday by train with my nan. There is no one like my mum I love her so much and she has been by my side every step on my long journey of mental health. I could never thank my mum enough. As I say she is my rock. Always has and always will be.

What a great day we have had going back to our roots. The Shard overlooks the hospital I was born in, thirty-eight years ago. I had a few beers and my mum had a few pink gins to celebrate. We even had pie, mash and liquor. Thanks MUM xxx

My recovery got better and better as the days went on. I write this book a few months later and I'm now due back to work any day now.

I just pray to God and have my fingers crossed, along with everything else crossed, that this never happens to me again.